Dedication

This book is dedicated to

THE 7 YEAR OLD ME

AND MY KIDS WHO HELP ME KEEP MY IMAGINATION AND SPIRIT YOUNG AND SUPPORT MY CRAZY IDEAS.

Mo & Kasey

BECCI HARRISON
THE DAYDREAMING UNICORN

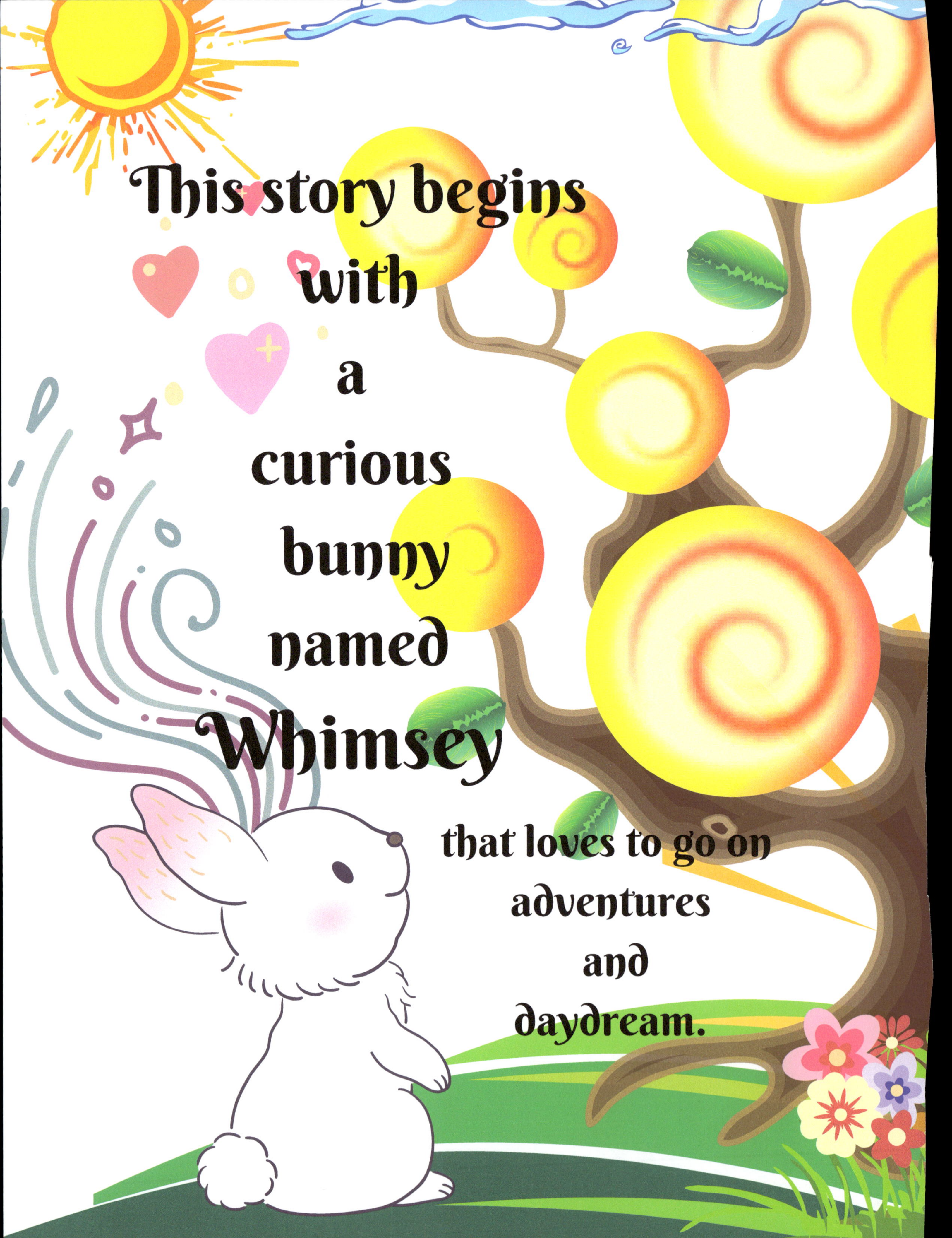

This story begins
with
a
curious
bunny
named
Whimsey
that loves to go on
adventures
and
daydream.

Whimsey lives in a magical land
with
tall majestic mountains.
BUCKET
OF
DREAMS

Whimesy travels the lands
hopping on the velvet green grass
or sliding on the sands of beaches
jumping on
giant rocks
and
boulders
Boop
Boop
Boop

Even hosting dance
parties in the
forest

There are lots of animal friends along the way,
some are new friends and

some are old friends,
always happy
to see
Whimsey
sharing the treasures in their life.

Always full of surprises!

The Oceans are full of vibrant colors
and
filled with strange sea life

and mysterious lands
under the water

that no one has ever visited.

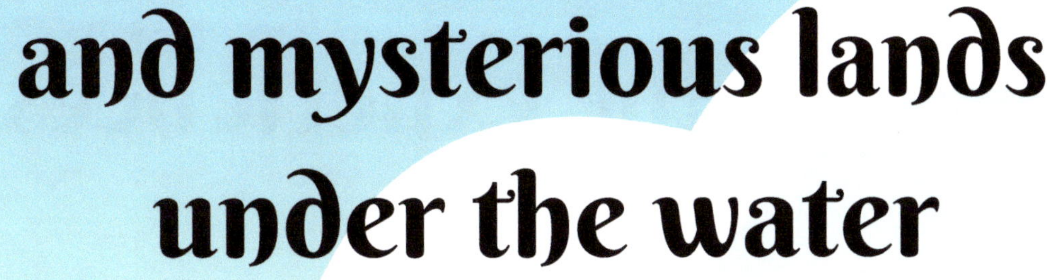

And along the way
Whimsey takes time to enjoy
all the experiences

whether
it is helping friends
with magic
MAGIC

or even relaxing

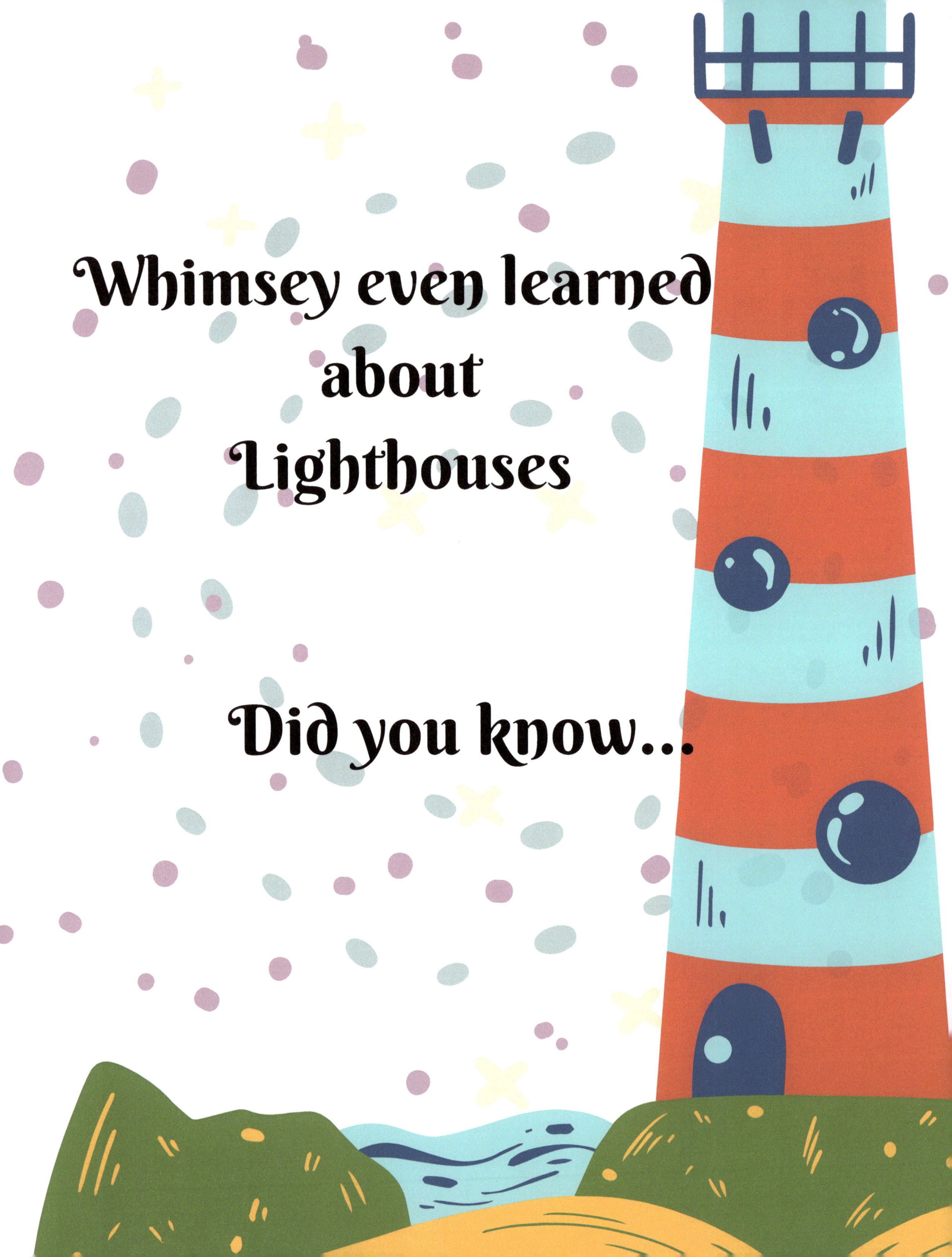

Whimsey even learned about Lighthouses

Did you know...

they help guide
vessels safely
into and out of harbors

Sometimes Unicorns
do too!!
(Shhhh, that's a secret)

Enjoying
a
windy
day
is
best

when you
can
fly a kite

or how about
a
balloon?
But, hold on
tight!

Pouncing through puddles
on a gentle rainy day
is one of Whimseys
favorite
experiences.

The rain is
falling
from the sky
it is feeding
all of the
beautiful trees
and
flowers and
filling the oceans and rivers

Along the way there are many things

Whimsey can enjoy,like picnics with friends filled with favorite snacks

or enjoying the company
of
friends along the way
to try new adventures

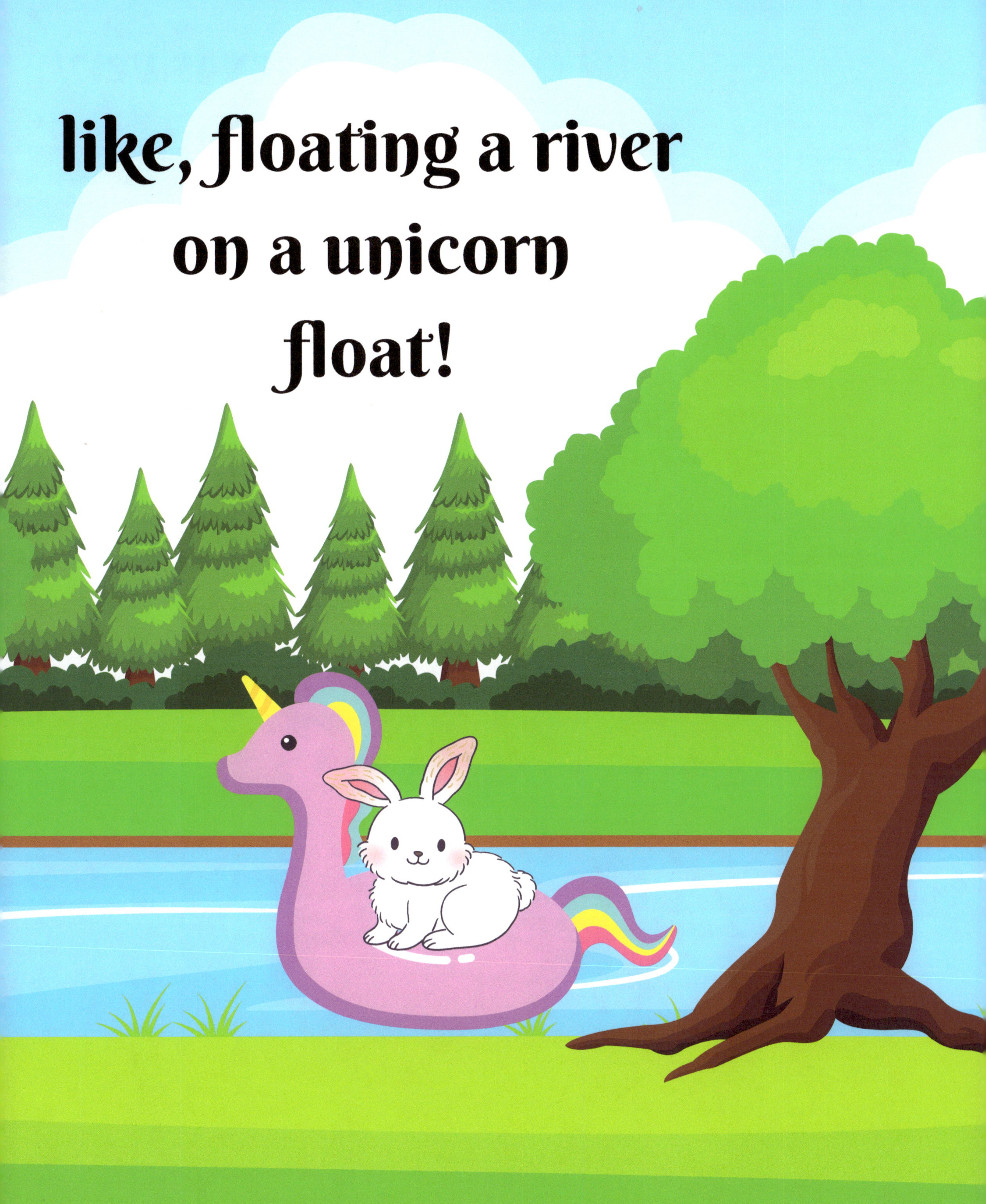
like, floating a river
on a unicorn
float!

Whimsey is very
curious
about
many
things
in
this
world

and enjoys
looking and hearing everything
that is around.
The birds chirping,
grasshoppers hopping
and
butterflies gently fluttering by

There are many adventures
to take advantage of
and
experience

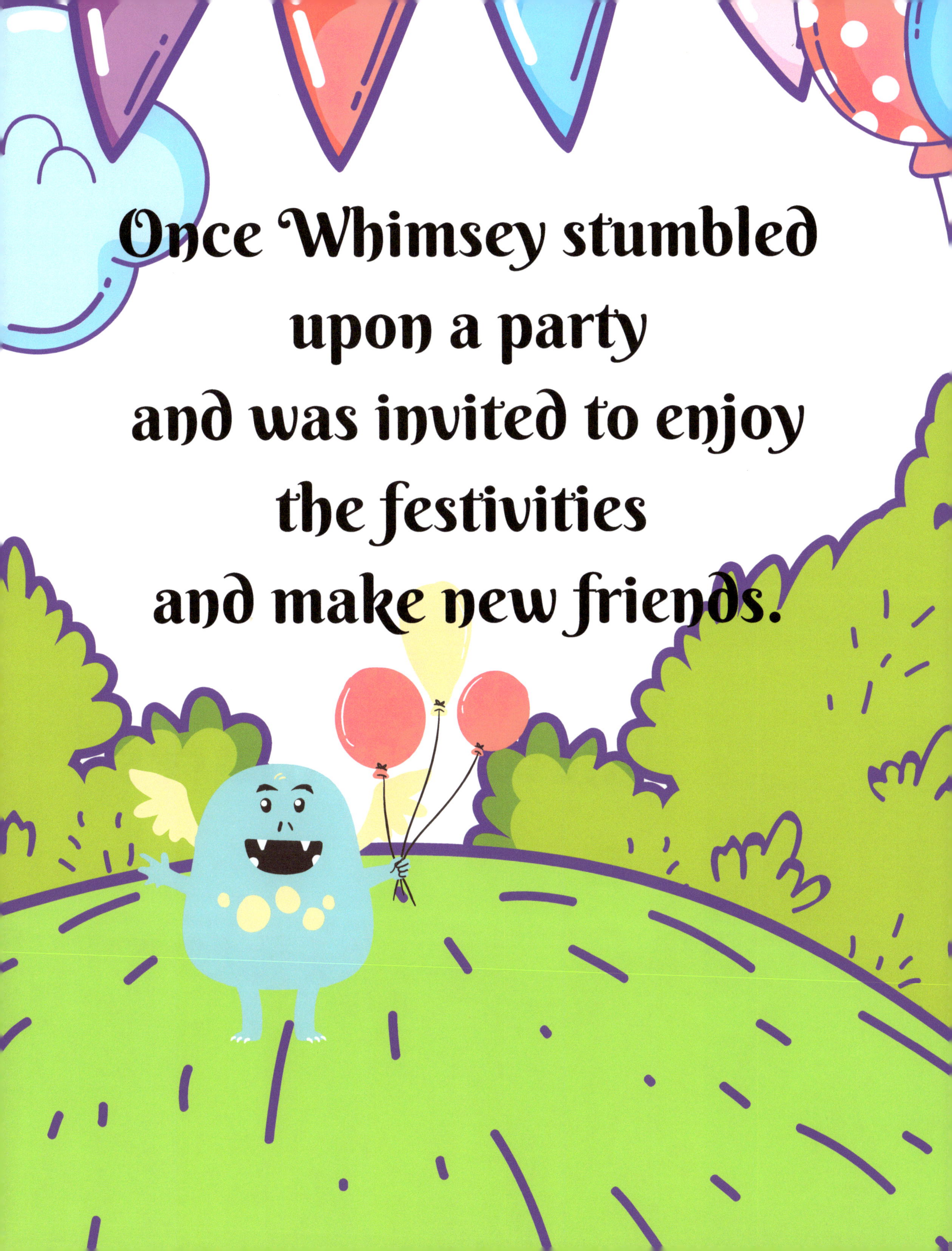

Once Whimsey stumbled
upon a party
and was invited to enjoy
the festivities
and make new friends.

Whimsey has never been afraid of new adventures

because experiencing
every moment
brings skills and
confidence

As the day turns to night,
the sky turns a darker shade of
blue and black,
stars start filling the sky
and
Mr. Moon peeps out.
It is time for
Whimsey and all his friends
to rest and recharge.

Boop
Boop
Boop
ZZZ
A new adventure awaits for tomorrow